The Importance of Obligatory Prayer and Fasting

SELECTION OF EXTRACTS AND PRAYERS
FROM THE BAHÁ'Í WRITINGS COMPILED BY
THE RESEARCH DEPARTMENT OF
THE UNIVERSAL HOUSE OF JUSTICE

Bahá'í Publications Australia

173 Mona Vale Road,
Ingleside, NSW, Australia 2101

Email: bpa@bahai.org.au
Website: www.bahaibooks.com

© 2000 Bahá'í Publications Australia
All rights reserved

First published 2000
Reprinted 2001

ISBN 1 876 322 96 9

DESIGNED BY FAIZI DESIGNS
PRINTED IN AUSTRALIA

Contents

One
FROM THE WRITINGS OF
BAHÁ'U'LLÁH ~ page 2

Two
FROM THE WRITINGS OF
'ABDU'L-BAHÁ ~ page 11

Three
PRAYERS BY BAHÁ'U'LLÁH
FOR THE FAST ~ page 23

NOTES ~ page 40

INDEX ~ page 41

The Universal House of Justice, in reviewing the further applicability of the laws of Bahá'u'lláh in the course of the past four years, determined that it is imperative for all Bahá'ís "to deepen their awareness of the blessings conferred by the laws which directly foster the devotional life of the individual and, thus, of the community." Among these laws are obligatory prayer and fasting which have been characterized by the Blessed Beauty as "two wings to man's life."

This present selection of newly authorized translations has been drawn from the vast ocean of the original Writings of Bahá'u'lláh and 'Abdu'l-Bahá. It is intended to further enhance the believers' insight into the far-reaching significance of these two great laws.
–May 2000

FROM THE WRITINGS OF BAHÁ'U'LLÁH

I   We, verily, have set forth all things in Our Book, as a token of grace unto those who have believed in God, the Almighty, the Protector, the Self-Subsisting. And We have ordained obligatory prayer and fasting so that all may by these means draw nigh unto God, the Most Powerful, the Well-Beloved. We have written down these two laws and expounded every irrevocable decree. We have forbidden men from following whatsoever might cause them to stray from the Truth, and have commanded them to observe that which will draw them nearer unto Him Who is the Almighty, the All-Loving. Say: Observe ye the commandments of God for love of His beauty, and be not of those who follow in the ways of the abject and foolish.

II   All praise be unto God, Who hath revealed the law of obligatory prayer as a reminder to His servants, and enjoined on them the Fast that those possessed of means may become apprised of the woes and sufferings of the destitute.

III   One who performeth neither good deeds nor acts of worship is like unto a tree which beareth no fruit, and an action which leaveth no trace. Whosoever experienceth the holy ecstasy of worship will refuse to barter such an act or any praise of God for all that existeth in the world. Fasting and obligatory prayer are as two wings to man's life. Blessed be the one who soareth with their aid in the heaven of the love of God, the Lord of all worlds.

IV. Cling firmly to obligatory prayer and fasting. Verily, the religion of God is like unto heaven; fasting is its sun, and obligatory prayer is its moon. In truth, they are the pillars of religion whereby the righteous are distinguished from those who transgress His commandments. We entreat God, exalted and glorified be He, that he may graciously enable all to observe that which He hath revealed in His Ancient Book.

V. Know thou that religion is as heaven; and fasting and obligatory prayer are its sun and its moon. We entreat God, exalted and glorified be He, to graciously aid everyone who acteth according to His will and good-pleasure.

VI. Be not neglectful of obligatory prayer and fasting. He who faileth to observe them hath not been nor will ever be acceptable in the sight of God. Follow ye wisdom under all conditions. He, verily, hath bidden all to observe that which hath been and will be of profit to them. He, in truth, is the All-Sufficing, the Most High.

VII As for obligatory prayer, it hath been sent down by the Pen of the Most High in such wise that it setteth ablaze the hearts and captivateth the souls and minds of men.

VIII Concerning obligatory prayer, it hath been revealed in such wise that whosoever reciteth it, even one time, with a detached heart, will find himself wholly severed from the world.

IX O My brother! How great, how very great, can the law of obligatory prayer be, when, through His mercy and loving kindness, one is enabled to observe it. When a man commenceth the recitation of the Obligatory Prayer, he should see himself severed from all created things and regard himself as utter nothingness before the will and purpose of God, in such wise that he seeth naught but Him in the world of being. This is the station of God's well-favored ones and those who are wholly devoted to Him. Should one perform the Obligatory Prayer in this manner, he will be accounted by God and the Concourse on high among those who have truly offered the prayer.

X. One of the deeds in obedience to the law is obligatory prayer. He Who is the Bearer of divine mysteries hath called it the ladder of ascent. He saith: "Obligatory prayer is a ladder of ascent for the believer." Within it are hidden and concealed a myriad effects and benefits. Indeed, they are beyond computation. How great would be a man's indolence and his injustice to himself if he were to abandon this ladder of ascent and attach himself to earthly treasures. It is our hope that we may be assisted to perform pure and acceptable deeds. We beseech God, exalted and glorified be He, to confirm us in that which He desireth and pleaseth and in that which will draw us nigh unto Him. Verily, He is the Almighty, the All-Powerful, He Who is wont to answer the prayers of all men.

XI. Of the new Obligatory Prayers that were later revealed, the long Obligatory Prayer should be said at those times when one feeleth himself in a prayerful mood. In truth, it hath been revealed in such wise that if it be recited to a rock, that rock would stir and speak forth; and if it be recited to a mountain, that mountain would move and flow. Well is it with the one who reciteth it and fulfilleth God's precepts. Whichever prayer is read will suffice.

XII We beseech God to assist His people that they may observe the most great and exalted Fast, which is to protect one's eye from beholding whatever is forbidden and to withhold one's self from food, drink and whatever is not of Him. We pray God to confirm His loved ones that they may succeed in accomplishing that which they have been commanded in this Day.

XIII Praise be unto Him Who hath revealed laws in accordance with His good-pleasure. Verily, He is sovereign over whatsoever He wisheth. O My friends! Act ye in accordance with what ye have been commanded in the Book. Fasting hath been decreed for you in the month of 'Ala. Fast ye for the sake of your Lord, the Mighty, the Most High. Restrain yourselves from sunrise to sunset. Thus doth the Beloved of mankind instruct you as bidden by God, the All-Powerful, the Unconstrained. It is not for anyone to exceed the limits laid down by God and His law, nor should anyone follow his own idle imaginings. Well is it with the one who fulfilleth My decrees for the love of My Beauty, and woe to the one who neglecteth the Dayspring of Command in the days of his Lord, the Almighty, the Omnipotent.

XIV. This is one of the nights of the Fast, and during it the Tongue of Grandeur and Glory proclaimed: There is no God beside Me, the Omnipotent Protector, the Self-Subsisting. We, verily, have commanded all to observe the Fast in these days as a bounty on Our part, but the people remain unaware, except for those who have attained unto the purpose of God as revealed in His laws and have comprehended His wisdom that pervadeth all things visible and invisible. Say: By God! His Law is a fortress unto you, could ye but understand. Verily, He hath no purpose therein save to benefit the souls of His servants, but, alas, the generality of mankind remain heedless thereof. Cling ye to the cord of God's laws, and follow not those who have turned away from the Book, for verily they have opposed God, the Mighty, the Beloved.

XV. These are the days of the Fast. Blessed is the one who through the heat generated by the Fast increaseth his love, and who, with joy and radiance, ariseth to perform worthy deeds. Verily, He guideth whomsoever He willeth to the straight path.

XVI *E*ven though outwardly the Fast is difficult and toilsome, yet inwardly it is bounty and tranquillity. Purification and training are conditioned and dependent only on such rigorous exercises as are in accord with the Book of God and sanctioned by Divine law, not those which the deluded have inflicted upon the people. Whatsoever God hath revealed is beloved of the soul. We beseech Him that He may graciously assist us to do that which is pleasing and acceptable unto Him.

XVII *V*erily, I say, fasting is the supreme remedy and the most great healing for the disease of self and passion.

XVIII *A*ll praise be to the one true God Who hath assisted His loved ones to observe the Fast and hath aided them to fulfill that which hath been decreed in the Book. In truth, ceaseless praise and gratitude are due unto Him for having graciously confirmed His loved ones to perform that which is the cause of the exaltation of His Word. If a man possessed ten thousand lives and offered them all to establish the truth of God's laws and commandments, he would still be beholden unto Him, since whatsoever proceedeth from His irresistible decree serveth solely to benefit His friends and loved ones.

XIX. There are various stages and stations for the Fast and innumerable effects and benefits are concealed therein. Well is it with those who have attained unto them.

XX. In clear cases of weakness, illness, or injury the law of the Fast is not binding. This injunction is in conformity with the precepts of God, eternal in the past, eternal in the future. Well is it with them who act accordingly.

XXI. The law of the Fast is ordained for those who are sound and healthy; as to those who are ill or debilitated, this law hath never been nor is now applicable.

TWO

FROM THE WRITINGS OF 'ABDU'L-BAHÁ

I. Obligatory prayer and fasting are among the most great ordinances of this holy Dispensation.

II. In the realm of worship, fasting and obligatory prayer constitute the two mightiest pillars of God's holy Law. Neglecting them is in no wise permitted, and falling short in their performance is of a certainty not acceptable. In the Tablet of Visitation He saith: "I beseech God, by Thee and by them whose faces have been illumined with the splendors of the light of Thy countenance, and who, for love of Thee, have observed all whereunto they were bidden." He declareth that observance of the commands of God deriveth from love for the beauty of the Best-Beloved. The seeker, when immersed in the ocean of the love of God, will be moved by intense longing and will arise to carry out the laws of God. Thus, it is impossible that a heart which containeth the fragrance of God's love should yet fail to worship Him, except under conditions when such an action would agitate the enemies and stir up dissension and mischief. Otherwise, a lover of the Abhá Beauty will assuredly and continually demonstrate perseverance in the worship of the Lord.

III   The laws of God regarding fasting and obligatory prayer are absolutely incumbent upon His servants. Therefore, they must turn their faces to the Point of Adoration of the celestial Concourse, hold fast to the most sublime Station, and pray and supplicate that they may be freed from the doubts of misinterpretation. This is the way of 'Abdu'l‑Bahá. This is the religion of 'Abdu'l‑Bahá. This is the path of 'Abdu'l‑Bahá. Whoever cherisheth the love of Bahá, let him choose this straight path. Whoever abandoneth this path, verily, he is of them who are shut out as by a veil from Him. Shouldst thou observe any soul who is in doubt about this commandment or who misinterpreteth it, but hath no secret motive or defiance in what he doeth, be friendly towards him, and with the utmost cordiality and through kind speech, endeavor to turn him from the path of such interpretation towards the plain meaning of the verses of God.

IV   The laws of God, such as fasting, obligatory prayer and the like, as well as His counsels regarding virtues, good deeds and proper conduct, must be carried out everywhere to the extent possible, unless some insurmountable obstacle or some great danger presents itself or it runneth counter to the dictates of wisdom. For indolence and laxity hinder the outpourings of love from the clouds of divine mercy, and people will thus remain deprived.

V. *O* ye loved ones of God! Out of gratitude for firmness in the eternal Covenant arise to serve the threshold of the omnipotent Lord, observe obligatory prayer and fasting, and spend your time in diffusing the sweet savors of God and in spreading the Divine verses. Tear asunder the veils, remove the obstacles, proffer the life-giving waters, and point out the path of salvation. This is what 'Abdu'l-Bahá admonisheth you every morn and eve.

VI. *O* thou daughter of the Kingdom! The Obligatory Prayers are binding inasmuch as they are conducive to humility and submissiveness, to setting one's face towards God and expressing devotion to Him. Through such prayer man holdeth communion with God, seeketh to draw near unto Him, converseth with the true Beloved of his heart, and attaineth spiritual stations.

VII. *O* thou spiritual friend! Thou hast asked about the wisdom of obligatory prayer. Know thou that such prayer is mandatory and binding. Man under no pretext whatsoever is excused from observing the prayer unless he is incapable of performing it or some great obstacle interveneth. The wisdom of obligatory prayer is this: That it causeth a connection between the servant and the True One, because at that time man with all his heart and soul turneth his face towards the Almighty, seeking His association and desiring His love and companionship. For a lover, there is no greater pleasure than to converse with his beloved, and for a seeker, there is no greater bounty than intimacy with the object of his desire. It is the greatest longing of every soul who is attracted to the Kingdom of God to find time to turn with entire devotion to his Beloved, so as to seek His bounty and blessing and immerse himself in the ocean of communion, entreaty and supplication. Moreover, obligatory prayer and fasting produce awareness and awakening in man, and are conducive to his protection and preservation from tests.

VIII *S*trengthen thou the foundation of the Faith of God, and worship the Almighty. Be constant in offering obligatory prayer, and be mindful of fasting. Day and night devote thyself to prayer, supplication and entreaty, especially at the prescribed times.

IX *T*he Obligatory Prayers have been set down by the Pen of the Most High and have been mentioned in the Persian "Questions and Answers", which supplementeth the Kitáb-i-Aqdas. They are clearly binding, and without a doubt everyone must perform one of these three prayers....

Through worship man becometh spiritual, his heart is attracted, and his soul and inner being attain such tenderness and exhilaration that the Obligatory Prayer instilleth new life in him. This is why in the Tablet of Visitation it hath been revealed: "I beseech God, by Thee and by them whose faces have been illumined with the splendors of the light of Thy countenance, and who, for love of Thee, have observed all whereunto they were bidden." It is clear then that love of the beauty of the All-Merciful impelleth one to the worship of Almighty God.

X *O* thou servant of God! Each morn God's infinite grace confirmeth the ardent and tearful invocations of 'Abdu'l-Bahá. Accordingly, let every awakened soul obtain, to the extent of its capacity, a portion of this spiritual grace. This can be achieved by fervently offering unto God prayers and supplications at every dawn and observing the law of obligatory prayer. Thus may his nostrils delight in the sweet savors wafting from the garden of the bounty of God, his soul attain new life, and his reality mirror forth the effulgences of the All-Merciful.

XI   Obligatory prayer causeth the heart to become attentive to the Divine kingdom. One is alone with God, converseth with Him, and acquireth bounties. Likewise, if one performeth the Obligatory Prayer with his heart in a state of utmost purity, he will obtain the confirmations of the Holy Spirit, and this will entirely obliterate love of self. I hope that thou wilt persevere in the recitation of the Obligatory Prayer, and thus will come to witness the power of entreaty and supplication.

XII   Thou hast written concerning obligatory prayer. Such prayer is binding and mandatory for everyone. Most certainly guide all to its observance, because it is like unto a ladder for the souls, a lamp unto the hearts of the righteous, and the water of life from the garden of paradise. It is a clear duty prescribed by the All-Merciful, in the observance of which it is in no wise permissible to be dilatory or neglectful.

XIII   Obligatory prayer and supplication cause man to reach the kingdom of mystery, and the worship of the Supreme One. They bestow nearness unto His threshold. There is a pleasure in offering prayers that transcendeth all other pleasures, and there is a sweetness in chanting and singing the verses of God which is the greatest desire of all the believers, men and women alike. While reciting the Obligatory

Prayer, one converseth intimately and shareth secrets with the true Beloved. No pleasure is greater than this, if one proceedeth with a detached soul, with tears overflowing, with a trusting heart and an eager spirit. Every joy is earthly save this one, the sweetness of which is divine.

XIV. Obligatory prayer is the very foundation of the Cause of God. Through it joy and vitality infuse the heart. Even if every grief should surround Me, as soon as I engage in conversing with God in obligatory prayer, all My sorrows disappear and I attain joy and gladness. A condition descendeth upon Me which I am unable to describe or express. Whenever, with full awareness and humility, we undertake to perform the Obligatory Prayer before God, and recite it with heartfelt tenderness, we shall taste such sweetness as to endow all existence with eternal life.

XV. Observe the Obligatory Prayer which is available to thee so that the gate of bounty may be opened and utmost spirituality attained; great signs will be witnessed and the spiritual ascent will be realized.

XVI   Persevere in the use of the Obligatory Prayer and early morning supplications, so that day by day thine awareness may increase, and, through the power of the knowledge of God, thou mayest rend asunder the veil of error of the people of doubt and lead them to His unfailing guidance. In every assembly, like unto a candle, thou shouldst give forth the light of Divine knowledge.

XVII   Recite the Obligatory Prayer and supplications as much as thou art able, so that day by day thou mayest attain to increased firmness and steadfastness and find greater joy and gladness. Thus the circle of divine knowledge will grow wider, and the fire of the love of God will burn brighter within thee.

XVIII   Obligatory prayers and supplications are the very water of life. They are the cause of existence, of the refinement of souls, and of their attainment to the utmost joy. Exercise the greatest care in this regard, and encourage others to recite the Obligatory Prayers and supplications.

XIX. O thou servant of the True Lord! Obligatory prayer and other supplications are essential to servitude unto Him Who is the All-Sufficing ... When the Obligatory Prayers and other prayers are joined together and follow each other, worship attaineth its perfection. It can be seen that these two are spiritual companions and are like one soul in two bodies. May God assist you all to thrive in love and fellowship.

XX. When saying the Obligatory Prayer, one must turn towards the Holy Reality of Bahá'u'lláh, that Reality which encompasseth all things.

XXI. As to the Obligatory Prayer, it hath a Qiblih that is fixed, specified, holy and blessed. I ask God that He may open the gate of the knowledge of this station to thine heart so that thou mayest apprehend whatever is necessary and proper, garner spiritual bounties from the heaven of the All-Merciful, obtain the effulgences of knowledge from the Sun of Reality, and become a manifestation of inspiration from the Unseen and a source of glad-tidings from the All-Merciful.

XXII   With regard to the Obligatory Prayer, this should be said individually, but it is not dependent on a private spot.

XXIII   O servant of the holy threshold! Thou hast asked about those prayers that are beyond what is prescribed, those that are recommended, invocations, and devotions honored by tradition. In this Dispensation that which hath been expressly prescribed is obligatory. But individual worship, invocations, supererogatory prayers, and specially recommended prayers are not binding. Nonetheless, the saying of any prayer individually after the Obligatory Prayers is well-pleasing and acceptable, but no particular ones have been singled out.

XXIV   Ordinances which are obligatory and decrees that are binding are those that have issued forth from the Supreme Pen or are issued by a decision of the Universal House of Justice. For we are the commanded, not the commander. We are the ones upon whom duties are imposed, not the ones who impose duties. This is the reality of the law of God and the foundation of the religion of God. As for devotions and invocations, whoever wisheth may, after the Obligatory Prayers, recite other supplications of the Blessed Perfection.

XXV   Thou hast written about the Fast. This is a most weighty matter and thou shouldst exert thine utmost in its observance. It is a fundamental of the Divine law, and one of the pillars of the religion of God.

XXVI   Well is it with you, as you have followed the Law of God and arisen to observe the Fast during these blessed days, for this physical fast is a symbol of the spiritual fast. This Fast leadeth to the cleansing of the soul from all selfish desires, the acquisition of spiritual attributes, attraction to the breezes of the All-Merciful, and enkindlement with the fire of divine love.

XXVII   Fasting is the cause of the elevation of one's spiritual station.

PRAYERS BY BAHÁ'U'LLÁH FOR THE FAST

I

This is, O my God, the first of the days on which Thou hast bidden Thy loved ones to observe the Fast. I ask of Thee by Thy Self and by him who hath fasted out of love for Thee and for Thy good-pleasure—and not out of self and desire, nor out of fear of Thy wrath—and by Thy most excellent names and august attributes, to purify Thy servants from the love of aught except Thee and to draw them nigh unto the Dawning-Place of the lights of Thy countenance and the Seat of the throne of Thy oneness. Illumine their hearts, O my God, with the light of Thy knowledge and brighten their faces with the rays of the Daystar that shineth from the horizon of Thy Will. Potent art Thou to do what pleaseth Thee. No God is there but Thee, the All-Glorious, Whose help is implored by all men.

Assist them, O my God, to render Thee victorious and to exalt Thy Word. Suffer them, then, to become as hands of Thy Cause amongst Thy servants, and make them to be revealers of Thy religion and Thy signs amongst mankind, in such wise that the whole world may be filled with Thy remembrance and praise and with Thy proofs and evidences. Thou art, verily, the All-Bounteous, the Most Exalted, the Powerful, the Mighty, and the Merciful.

II

In the Name of Him Who hath been promised in the Books of God, the All-Knowing, the All-Informed! The days of fasting have arrived wherein those servants who circle round Thy throne and have attained Thy presence have fasted. Say: O God of names and creator of heaven and earth! I beg of Thee by Thy Name, the All-Glorious, to accept the fast of those who have fasted for love of Thee and for the sake of Thy good-pleasure and have carried out what Thou hast bidden them in Thy Books and Tablets. I beseech Thee by them to assist me in the promotion of Thy Cause and to make me steadfast in Thy love, that my footsteps may not slip on account of the clamor of Thy creatures. Verily, Thou art powerful over whatsoever Thou willest. No God is there but Thee, the Quickener, the All-Powerful, the Most Bountiful, the Ancient of Days.

III   *P*raise be unto Thee, O Lord my God! We have observed the Fast in conformity with Thy bidding and break it now through Thy love and Thy good-pleasure. Deign to accept, O my God, the deeds that we have performed in Thy path wholly for the sake of Thy beauty with our faces set towards Thy Cause, free from aught else but Thee. Bestow, then, Thy forgiveness upon us, upon our forefathers, and upon all such as have believed in Thee and in Thy mighty signs in this most great, this most glorious Revelation. Potent art Thou to do what Thou choosest. Thou art, verily, the Most Exalted, the Almighty, the Unconstrained.

IV   *O* my God and my Master! Thou seest me among Thy creatures who have rebelled and transgressed against Thee. Every time I invite them unto the ocean of Thy knowledge, their repudiation of Thy Cause increaseth and their rejection of the Dawning-Place of Thy Will waxeth greater. I beg of Thee, O my God, by those who have fasted for love of Thee and have quaffed the living waters of submission from the hands of Thy bounty, to ordain for Thy loved ones, who under the blaze of the orb of Thy trials have clung to the cord of patience, all the good Thou hast reckoned in Thy Books and Thy Tablets. Write down, then, for such as have been afflicted with adversities for Thy sake, the reward of those who have suffered martyrdom in the path of Thy good-pleasure. Send down, moreover, upon them, O Lord, that which will rejoice their hearts, solace their eyes, and exhilarate their souls. Thou art, verily, the Most Powerful, the Most Exalted, the Help in Peril, the All-Knowing, the All-Wise.

*P*raised be Thou, O God, my God! These are the days whereon Thou hast enjoined Thy chosen ones, Thy loved ones and Thy servants to observe the Fast, which Thou hast made a light unto the people of Thy kingdom, even as Thou didst make obligatory prayer a ladder of ascent unto those who acknowledge Thy unity. I beg of Thee, O my God, by these two mighty pillars, which Thou hast ordained as a glory and honor for all mankind, to keep Thy religion safe from the mischief of the ungodly and the plotting of every wicked doer. O Lord, conceal not the light which Thou hast revealed through Thy strength and Thine omnipotence. Assist, then, those who truly believe in Thee with the hosts of the seen and the unseen by Thy command and Thy sovereignty. No God is there but Thee, the Almighty, the Most Powerful.

VI

*E*xalted art Thou, O Lord my God! I beseech Thee by those whom Thou hast bidden to observe the Fast for the sake of Thy love and good-pleasure, who have demonstrated their allegiance to Thy law and followed Thy verses and precepts, and who have broken their fast while enjoying near access to Thee and beholding Thy countenance. By Thy glory! Since they are turning to the court of Thy good-pleasure, all their days are days of fasting. Were the mouth of Thy will to address them saying: "Observe, for My beauty's sake, the fast, O people, and set no limit to its duration," I swear by the majesty of Thy glory, that every one of them will faithfully observe it, will abstain from whatsoever will violate Thy law, and will continue to do so until they yield up their souls unto Thee, for they have tasted the sweetness of Thy call, and become inebriated with Thy remembrance and praise and with the words proceeding from the lips of Thy command.

I beseech Thee, O Lord, by Thyself, the Exalted, the Most High, and by Thy Latter Manifestation through Whom the kingdom of names and the dominion of attributes have been convulsed, and the inhabitants of earth and heaven became intoxicated, and all who dwell in the realms of Revelation and creation trembled except such as have fasted from all that is repugnant to Thy good-pleasure and restrained themselves from turning toward aught besides Thee, to include us among them and to write down our names on the Tablet whereon Thou hast inscribed their names. O God, through the wonders of Thy might and the tokens of Thy sovereignty and grandeur, Thou didst send forth their names from out of the sea of Thy names, and didst create their inner essences out of the substance of Thy love, and their inmost beings from the spirit of Thy Cause. Theirs is a reunion not succeeded by separation, a nearness that knoweth no remoteness, and a perpetuity that hath no end. Verily, these are servants who ever recount Thee, who eternally circle round Thee, and who circumambulate the sanctuary of Thy presence and the Kaaba of reunion with Thee. Thou hast ordained, O my God, no distinction between them and Thee, except that when they beheld the lights of Thy countenance, they set their faces towards Thee, and prostrated themselves before Thy beauty, submissive to Thy greatness and severed from all things besides Thee.

We have fasted this day, O my Lord, by Thy command and Thy bidding in accordance with what Thou hast revealed in Thy perspicuous Book. We have withheld our souls from passion and from whatsoever Thou abhorest until the day drew to an end and the time arrived to break the Fast. Wherefore, I implore Thee, O Desire of the hearts of ardent lovers and Beloved of the souls of them who are endued with understanding, O Rapture of the breasts of them that yearn after Thee and Object of the desire of them that seek Thee, to cause us to soar in the atmosphere of Thy nearness and the heaven of Thy presence, and to accept from us what we have performed in the pathway of Thy love and good-pleasure. Write down our names, then, among those who have acknowledged Thy oneness and confessed to Thy singleness and who have humbled themselves before the evidences of Thy majesty and the tokens of Thy grandeur, those who have taken refuge in Thy nearness and sought shelter in Thee, who have expended their lives in their eagerness to meet Thee and attain the court of Thy presence, and who have cast the world behind their backs for love of Thee and severed every tie with aught save Thee in their eagerness to draw nigh unto Thee. These are servants whose hearts melt in ardent desire for Thy beauty at the mention of Thy Name, and whose eyes overflow with tears in their longing to find Thee and enter the precincts of Thy court.

This is, O my Lord, my tongue which testifieth to Thy unity and peerlessness, mine eye which beholdeth the seat of Thy generosity and manifold bounties, and mine ear which is ready to hearken unto Thy summons and Thine utterance, for I am assured, O my God, that Thou hast decreed the words proceeding out of the mouth of Thy will to be inexhaustible, and unto them the ears which Thou hast sanctified to hear Thy words and verses are at all times hearkening. And these are my hands, O my Lord, uplifted toward the heaven of Thy favor and tender mercy. Wilt Thou, then, turn away this poor one who hath taken to himself no beloved except Thee, no bestower beside Thee, nor king other than Thee, no shelter save beneath the shadow of Thy mercy, and no refuge but before Thy gate, which Thou hast opened unto all who dwell in Thy heaven and on Thine earth? Nay, by Thy glory! I am he whose confidence in Thy loving kindness will remain undaunted even though Thou wert to afflict me with torments for the duration of Thy dominion; and should anyone ask me about Thee, every limb of my body would proclaim: "He is beloved in His acts and obeyed in His decree, merciful in His nature and compassionate to His creatures!"

Thy might beareth me witness, O Well-Beloved of the hearts of them that yearn after Thee, wert Thou to turn me away from Thy door and abandon me to the swords of the tyrants amongst Thy servants and to the rods of the ungodly amongst Thy creatures, and should someone ask me about Thee, every hair of my body would still declare: "He is, in truth, the Best Beloved of the worlds; He is the Most Bountiful; He is the Ever-Abiding! He draweth me nigh whilst distancing me from Himself; He granteth me His sanctuary whilst debarring me from His presence. None found I more merciful than He, by Whom I have become independent of all else but Him and have been raised up above aught besides Himself."

Well is it with the one, O my God, who hath been so enriched by Thee as to be made independent of the kingdoms of earth and heaven. Rich is the one who hath held fast to the cord of Thy wealth, is submissive before Thy face, and for whom Thou art sufficient above all things. Poor is the one who hath dispensed with Thee, waxed proud before Thee, turned away from Thy presence, and disbelieved in Thy signs. Suffer me, then, O my God and my Beloved, to be numbered with those whom the breezes of Thy will move as they list, not with those whom the wind of self and passion stirreth and directeth as it pleaseth. No God is there but Thee, the Almighty, the Exalted, the Most Bountiful.

All glory be to Thee, O my God, for Thou hast graciously enabled me to fast during this month which Thou hast related to Thy Name, the Most Exalted, and called 'Ala (Loftiness). Thou hast commanded that Thy servants and Thy people should fast therein and seek thereby to draw nearer unto Thee. The days and months of the year have culminated with the Fast, even as the first month began with Thy Name, Bahá, that all might testify that Thou art the First and the Last, the Manifest and the Hidden, and be well assured that the glory of all names is conferred only through the glory of Thy Cause and the word expounded by Thy will and revealed through Thy purpose. Thou hast ordained that this month be a remembrance and honor from Thee, and a sign of Thy presence amongst them, that they may not forget Thy grandeur and Thy majesty, Thy sovereignty and Thy glory, and may be well assured that from time immemorial Thou hast ever been and wilt ever be Ruler over the entire creation. Nothing created in the heavens or on the earth can hinder Thee in Thy governance, nor can anyone in the realms of Revelation and creation prevent Thee from fulfilling Thy purpose.

I implore Thee, O my God, by Thy name whereby all the kindreds of the earth have wailed, except such as Thou hast safeguarded with Thine unerring protection and sheltered beneath the shadow of Thy transcendent mercy, to make us so firm in Thy Cause and steadfast in Thy love that were Thy servants to rise up against Thee and Thy people turn away from Thee, and no one would remain on earth to invoke Thy name or set his face toward the sanctuary of communion with Thee and the Kaaba of Thy sanctity, I would still arise singly and alone to render Thy Cause victorious, to exalt Thy word, to proclaim Thy sovereignty, and to celebrate the praise of Thine august Self. And this, O Lord, even though each time I venture to extol Thee by any name, I am filled with perplexity, for I am fully aware that all of Thine exalted attributes and all of the most excellent names which I associate with Thee and by which in Thy holy presence I supplicate Thee, reflect naught but the measure of mine own understanding, inasmuch as whenever I have regarded a name to be laudable, I have associated it with Thyself.

Immeasurably exalted is Thy true state above the description or knowledge of anyone besides Thee, and sanctified art Thou from the glorification of Thy creatures and the praise of Thy servants in their attempts to ascend unto Thee. Whatsoever appeareth from Thy servants is limited by the limitations of their own selves and is created by their own idle fancies and imaginings.

Alas, alas, O my Beloved, for mine inability to befittingly praise Thee and for my shortcomings during Thy days! If I acclaim Thee, O my God, as Him Who knoweth all things, I readily perceive that shouldst Thou point to a mute rock with a single finger of Thy will, Thou wouldst enable it to unfold the knowledge of all past and future ages; and if I extol Thee as the All-Powerful, I find that one word issuing from the mouth of Thy purpose is sufficient to convulse the heavens and the earth.

Thy glory beareth me witness, O Beloved of all that recognize Thee, should any learned one fail to confess his ignorance before the revelations of Thy knowledge, he would be accounted the most ignorant of Thy people; and should any mighty one refuse to admit his weakness before the evidences of Thy power, he would be considered the weakest and the most heedless of Thy creatures. Given my knowledge and certainty that this is so, how can I extol Thee or describe and praise Thee? Wherefore, knowing my weakness, I have hastened toward the shelter of Thy strength; and realizing my poverty, I have sought refuge under the shadow of Thy wealth; and recognizing my powerlessness, I have arisen to stand before the tabernacle of Thy power and might. Wilt thou cast away this poor one after he hath taken no one but Thee as his succorer, or turn away this stranger after he hath found no one but Thee to be his true beloved?

Thou knowest all that is in me, O Lord, but I know not what is in Thee. Have mercy then upon me through Thy loving providence and inspire me with that which shall give peace to my heart during Thy days and tranquillity to my soul through the revelations of Thy sacred presence. All created things have been illumined with the splendors of the lights of Thy countenance, O Lord, and the dwellers of earth and heaven are shining resplendently on account of the manifestations of Thine incomparable majesty, in such wise that I behold nothing without first beholding within it the revelation of Thyself, a revelation which is hidden from the sight of those among Thy servants who lie fast asleep.

Deprive me not, O my Lord, of Thy grace which hath encompassed all the realms of existence, whether visible or invisible. Wilt Thou stay far removed, O my God, after Thou hast invited all mankind to return and draw nigh unto Thee, and urged them to hold fast to Thy cord? Wilt Thou cast me out, O my Beloved, even when Thou hast promised in Thine incorruptible Book and in Thy wondrous verses to gather all those who yearn after Thee within the pavilion of Thy gracious providence, and those who desire Thee under the shadow of Thy bountiful favor, and those who search for Thee under the canopy of Thy mercy and loving-kindness?

I swear by Thy might, O my God, that my lamentations have constrained my Pen, and, verily, the cry of my heart hath seized the reins from my hands. At whatever time I reassure myself and gladden my soul with the wonders of Thy mercy, the tokens of Thy gracious providence, and the evidences of Thy generosity, I tremble before the manifestations of Thy justice and the signs of Thy wrath. I recognize that Thou art known by these two names and described by these two attributes, yet Thou carest not whether Thou art invoked by Thy name the Ever-Forgiving, or Thy name the Wrathful.

By Thy glory, were it not for my knowledge that Thy mercy surpasseth all things, the limbs of my body would have ceased to exist, my reality been extinguished and my inner being reduced to utter nothingness. But when I behold that Thy grace encompasseth all things and Thy mercy embraceth the entire creation, my soul and my inmost being become well assured.

Alas, alas, O my God, for the things that have escaped me during Thy days, and again alas, alas, O Desire of my heart, for what I have left undone in service and obedience to Thee during these days the likes of which the eyes of Thy chosen ones and trusted ones have never witnessed! I entreat Thee, O my Lord, by Thy Self and by the Manifestation of Thy Cause Who is seated upon the throne of Thy mercy, to confirm me in Thy service and good-pleasure. Guard me, then, from those who have turned away from Thee and disbelieved in Thy verses, who have denied Thy truth, resisted Thine evidences, and violated Thy Covenant and testament.

All praise, O Lord my God, be unto Him Who is the Manifestation of Thine Essence, the Dayspring of Thy oneness, the Mine of Thy knowledge, the Source of Thy Revelation, the Repository of Thine inspiration, the Seat of Thy sovereignty, and the Dawning-Place of Thy Divinity—He Who is the

Primal Point, the Most Exalted Countenance, the Ancient Root, and the Quickener of nations; and glory be upon him who was the first to believe in Him and in His verses, whom Thou didst make a throne for the ascendancy of Thy most sublime Word, a focal-point for the manifestation of Thy most excellent names, a dayspring of the radiance of the Sun of Thy providence, a dawning-place for the appearance of Thy names and attributes, and a treasury of the pearls of Thy wisdom and Thy commandments. And all honor be upon him who was the last to come unto Him, whose arrival was like His arrival, and Thy manifestation in him like Thy manifestation in Him , except that he was illumined with the lights of His face and prostrated himself before Him and testified to his servitude unto Him; and glory be upon those who were martyred in His path and who offered up their lives for love of His beauty.

We testify, O my God, that these are servants who have believed in Thee and in Thy signs, who have sought the sanctuary of Thy presence and turned toward Thy countenance, who have directed their faces toward the court of Thy nearness and walked in the path of Thy good-pleasure, who have worshipped Thee according to Thy desire and detached themselves from all but Thee. O Lord, confer upon their spirits and their bodies at all times a share of the wonders of Thine all-encompassing mercy. Thou art, verily, powerful to do as Thou pleaseth. No God is there save Thee, the Almighty, the All-Glorious, Whose help is implored by all men.

I beseech Thee, O Lord, by Him and by them, and by Him Whom Thou hast established on the throne of Thy Faith and caused to overshadow all the dwellers of earth and heaven, to purify us from our transgressions, to ordain for us a seat of truth in Thy presence and to cause us to associate with those whom the adversities of the world and its misfortunes have not hindered from turning toward Thee. Thou art, verily, the All-Powerful, the Most Exalted, the Protector, the Ever-Forgiving, the Most Merciful.

NOTES

1. A tradition attributed to the Imám 'Alí

2. "I beseech God ... were bidden," translated by Shoghi Effendi; see Prayers and Meditations by Bahá'u'lláh, CLXXX

3. Ibid.

4. " 'Observe, for My Beauty's sake' ... souls unto Thee," translated by Shoghi Effendi; see Gleanings from the Writings of Bahá'u'lláh, CLX

5. Mullá Ḥusayn

6. Quddús

7. Idem

8. The Báb

INDEX

	TOPIC	PAGE-REFERENCE
A	'Abdu'l-Bahá	11
B	Bahá'u'lláh	1, 23
	believers	17-XIII
C	capacity	16-X
	chanting	17-XIII
	chosen ones	27-V, 37-IV
	confirmations	17-XI
	Covenant	14-V, 37-IV
D	dawn	16-X,
	deeds	2-III, 5-X, 7-XV, 13-IV, 26-III
	devotions	21-XXIII, 21-XXIV
	dissension and mischief	12-II
	drink	6-XII
E	earthly treasures	5-X
	eternal life	18-XIV
F	Fast	2-II, 6-XII, 6-XIII, 7-XV, 8-XVI, 9-XIX, 9-XX, 9-XXI, 22-XXV, 22-XXVII, 25-I
	fasting	2-I, 2-III, 3-IV, 3-VI, 6-XIII, 8-XVII, 12-I, 12-II, 13-III, 13-IV, 14-V, 15-V11, 15-VIII, 22-XXVII, 25-II, 29-VI
	food	6-XII
	forbidden	2-I, 6-XII

G	God	2-I, 2-II, 2-III, 3-IV, 3-V, 3-VI, 4-IX, 5-X, 5-XI, 6-XII, 6-XIII, 7-XIV, 8-XVI, 9-XX, 12-II, 13-III, 13-IV, 14-V, 14-VI, 15-VII, 15-VIII, 16-IX, 16-X, 17-XI, 17-XIII, 18-XIV, 19-XVI, 19-XVII, 20-XIX, 20-XXI, 21-XXIV, 22-XXV, 24-I, 25-II, 26-III, 26-IV, 27-V, 28-VI, 29-V1, 30-VI, 32-VI, 33-VI, 34-VI, 36-VI, 37-VI, 38-VI
	grief	18-XIV
H	healing	8-XVII
	Holy Spirit	17-XI
	humility	14-VI, 18-XIV
I	idle imaginings	6-XIII
	illness	9-XX
	indolence	5-X, 13-IV
	injury	9-XX
	injustice to himself	5-X
	inspiration	20-XXI, 38-VI
	invocations	16-X, 21-XXIII, 21-XXIV
J	joy	7-XV, 18-XIV, 19-XVII, 19-XVIII
K	Kitáb-i-Aqdas	15-IX
	knowledge	19-XVI, 19-XVII, 20-XXI, 24-I, 26-IV, 35-VI, 36-VI, 37-VI
L	Law	2-II, 4-IX, 5-X, 6-XIII, 7-XIV, 8-XVI, 9-XX, 9-XXI, 11-XXIV, 12-II, 21-XXIV, 22-XXV, 22-XXVI, 28-VI
	laws (ordinances)	2-I, 6-XIII, 7-XIV, 8-XVIII, 12-II, 13-111, 13-IV

	love	2-I, 3-III, 6-XIII, 7-XIV, 12-II, 13-III, 13-IV, 15-VII, 16-IX, 17-XI, 19-XVII, 20-XIX, 22-XXVI, 24-1, 26-III, 27-III, 27-IV, 28-VI, 29-VI, 30-VI, 33-VI, 38-VI
M	mankind	6-XIII, 7-XIV, 24-1, 27-V, 36-VI
	mercy	4-IX, 13-IV, 31-VI, 33-VI, 35-VI, 36-VI, 37-VI, 38-VI
N	near access	28-VI
	nights of the Fast	7-XIV
	new life	16-IX, 16-X
O	obligatory prayer	2-I, 2-II, 2-III, 3-IV, 3-V, 3-VI, 4-VIII, 4-IX, 5-X, 5-XI, 12-I, 12-II, 13-III, 13-IV, 14-V, 14-VI, 14-VII, 15-VIII, 15-IX, 16-X, 17-XI, 17-XII, 17-XIII, 18-XIV, 18-XV, 19-XVI, 19-XVII, 20-XIX, 20-XX, 20-XXI, 21-XXII, 21-XXIII, 27-V
	obstacle	14-VII
P	passion	8-XVII, 29-VI, 32-VI
	pleasure	15-VII, 17-XIII
	power	17-XI, 19-XVI, 35-VI
	prayer/prayers	4-IX, 5-X, 5-XI, 14-VI, 14-VII, 15-VIII, 15-IX, 16-X, 17-XII, 17-XIII, 20-XIX, 21-XXIII
	protection	15-VII, 33-VI,
	prescribed times	15-VIII
	purity	17-XI
Q	Qiblih	20-XXI

R	recitation	17-XI
	religion	3-IV, 3-V, 13-III, 21-XXIV, 22-XXV, 24-I, 27-V
	righteous	3-IV, 17-XII
S	salvation	14-V
	seeker	12-II, 15-VII
	self	6-XII, 8-XVII, 17-XI, 24-1, 32-VI
	servitude	20-XIX, 38-VI
	spiritual	14-VI, 14-VII, 16-IX, 18-XV, 20-XIX, 20-XXI, 22-XXVI, 22-XXVII,
	spirituality	18-XV
	soul/souls	4-VII, 7-XIV, 8-XVI, 13-III, 14-VII, 16-IX, 16-X, 12-II, 18-XIII, 19-XVIII, 20-XIX, 22-XXVI, 27-IV, 29-VI, 36-VI, 37-VI
	station	4-IX, 9-XIX, 13-III, 14-VI, 22-XXVII
	steadfastness	19-XVII
	supplications	16-X, 19-XVI, 19-XVII, 20-XIX, 21-XXIV
T	Tablet of Visitation	12-II, 16-IX
	tests	15-VII
	training	8-XVI
U	Universal House of Justice	21-XXIV
V	virtues	13-IV
	violated Thy Covenant	37-VI

W	weakness	9-XX, 36-VI
	wisdom	3-VI, 7-XIV, 13-IV, 14-VII, 38-VI
	Word	8-XVIII, 24-1, 38-VI, 39-VI
	world	2-III, 4-VIII, 4-IX, 24-1, 30-VI, 39-VI
	worship	2-III, 12-II, 15-VIII, 16-IX, 17-XIII, 20-XIX, 21-XXIII
Y	yearn	30-VI, 31-VI, 36-VI

Other compilations from the Universal House of Justice

Bahá'í Consultation
Bahá'í Education
Centres of Bahá'í Learning
Constitution of the Universal House of Justice
A Chaste and Holy Life
Covenant
Continental Board of Counsellors
Conservation of Earth's Resources
Divorce
Excellence in All Things
Family Life
Heaven of Divine Wisdom
Health and Healing
Issues Relating to Community Functioning
Life Blood of the Cause
Living the Life
Local Spiritual Assembly
National Spiritual Assembly
Nineteen Day Feast
National Convention
Ocean of My Words
Onward March of the Faith
Peace
Power of Divine Assistance
Prayer, Meditation and Devotional Attitude
Promoting Entry by Troops
Preserving Bahá'í Marriages
Special Measure of Love
Spiritual Foundations
Social and Economic Development
Scholarship
Teaching the Bahá'í Faith
Teaching Prominent People
Trustworthiness
Universal House of Justice
Women
Youth

Available from Bahá'í Publications Australia
173 Mona Vale Road, Ingleside, NSW 2101, Australia
Email: bpa@bahai.org.au

For more information on these and other titles, please visit our website
www.bahaibooks.com